AARON JUDGE

CHARLIE BEATTIE

WWW.APEXEDITIONS.COM

Copyright © 2026 by Apex Editions, Mendota Heights, MN 55120. All rights reserved. No part of this book may be reproduced or utilized in any form or by any means without written permission from the publisher.

Apex is distributed by North Star Editions:
sales@northstareditions.com | 888-417-0195

Produced for Apex by Red Line Editorial.

Photographs ©: Kyodo/AP Images, cover, 1; Bailey Orr/Texas Rangers/ Getty Images Sport/Getty Images, 4–5; LM Otero/AP Images, 6–7, 58–59; Shutterstock Images, 8–9, 10–11; Loren Orr/Getty Images Sport/Getty Images, 12–13; Josh Holmberg/Cal Sport Media/AP Images, 14–15; Jeff Zelevansky/Getty Images Sport/Getty Images, 16–17; Brian Westerholt/Four Seam Images/AP Images, 18–19; Tomasso DeRosa/AP Images, 20–21; Brace Hemmelgarn/Minnesota Twins/Getty Images Sport/Getty Images, 22–23; Mike Janes/Four Seam Images/AP Images, 24–25; Rich Schultz/ Getty Images Sport/Getty Images, 27, 30–31; Rob Leiter/MLB Photos/Getty Images Sport/Getty Images, 28–29; Jim McIsaac/Getty Images Sport/Getty Images, 32–33, 38–39; Al Bello/Getty Images Sport/Getty Images, 34–35; Abbie Parr/Getty Images Sport/Getty Images, 36–37; Paul Bereswill/Getty Images Sport/Getty Images, 40–41; Sarah Stier/Getty Images Sport/Getty Images, 42–43; Vaughn Ridley/Getty Images Sport/Getty Images, 44–45; Justin Casterline/Getty Images Sport/Getty Images, 46–47; Mike Stobe/ Getty Images Sport/Getty Images, 49; G. Fiume/Getty Images Sport/Getty Images, 50–51; New York Yankees/Getty Images Sport/Getty Images, 52–53; Justin Casterline/Getty Images Sport/Getty Images, 54–55; Alex Slitz/Getty Images Sport/Getty Images, 56–57

Library of Congress Control Number: 2024952004

ISBN
979-8-89250-723-3 (hardcover)
979-8-89250-775-2 (paperback)
979-8-89250-757-8 (ebook pdf)
979-8-89250-741-7 (hosted ebook)

Printed in the United States of America
Mankato, MN
082025

NOTE TO PARENTS AND EDUCATORS

Apex books are designed to build literacy skills in striving readers. Exciting, high-interest content attracts and holds readers' attention. The text is carefully leveled to allow students to achieve success quickly.

TABLE OF CONTENTS

CHAPTER 1
SMASHING A RECORD 4

CHAPTER 2
CALIFORNIA KID 8

CHAPTER 3
ROAD TO THE MAJORS 16

IN THE SPOTLIGHT
A GRAND ENTRANCE 26

CHAPTER 4
TOP TALENT 28

CHAPTER 5
MAKING HISTORY 38

IN THE SPOTLIGHT
WALK-OFF CLINCHER 48

CHAPTER 6
ALL RISE 50

TIMELINE • 58
COMPREHENSION QUESTIONS • 60
GLOSSARY • 62
TO LEARN MORE • 63
ABOUT THE AUTHOR • 63
INDEX • 64

CHAPTER 1

SMASHING A RECORD

Aaron Judge towered over home plate. The New York Yankees slugger held his bat high. The 2022 season was almost over. And Judge hoped to make history. On the mound, the pitcher wound up to throw. The ball sped toward Judge.

The New York Yankees played the Texas Rangers on October 4, 2022.

Judge crushed the pitch. The ball sailed over the fence in left field. Even fans from the other team cheered as Judge rounded the bases. It was his 62nd home run of the season. The Yankees dugout emptied. The players celebrated at home plate. Judge's home run set a new American League (AL) record. The previous mark had stood since 1961.

THE TRUE CHAMP?
Aaron Judge wasn't the first to hit 62 homers in a season. Three National League (NL) players did it before him. But those three players were linked to steroid use. So, many fans consider Judge the true record holder.

Aaron Judge's 62nd home run traveled 391 feet (119 m).

CHAPTER 2

CALIFORNIA KID

Aaron Judge was born on April 26, 1992. Soon after, he was adopted by two teachers named Patty and Wayne. Aaron grew up in Linden, California.

Linden is a small town in central California. It is surrounded by many farms.

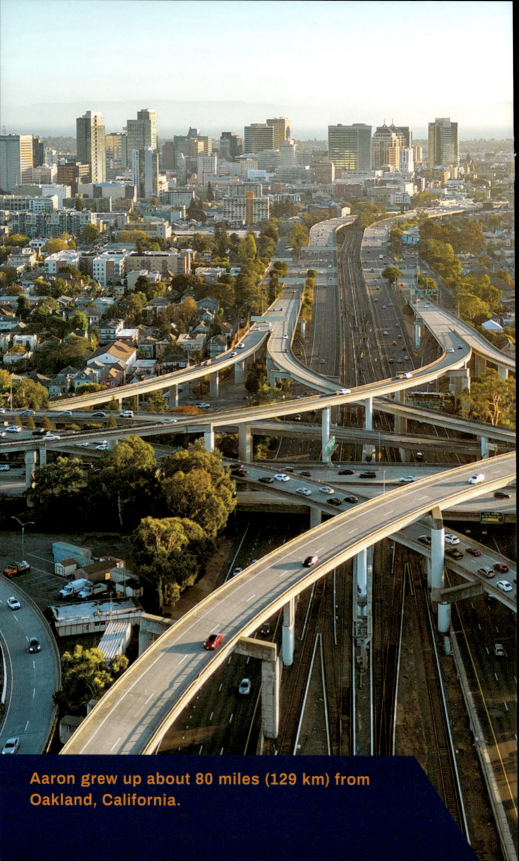

Aaron grew up about 80 miles (129 km) from Oakland, California.

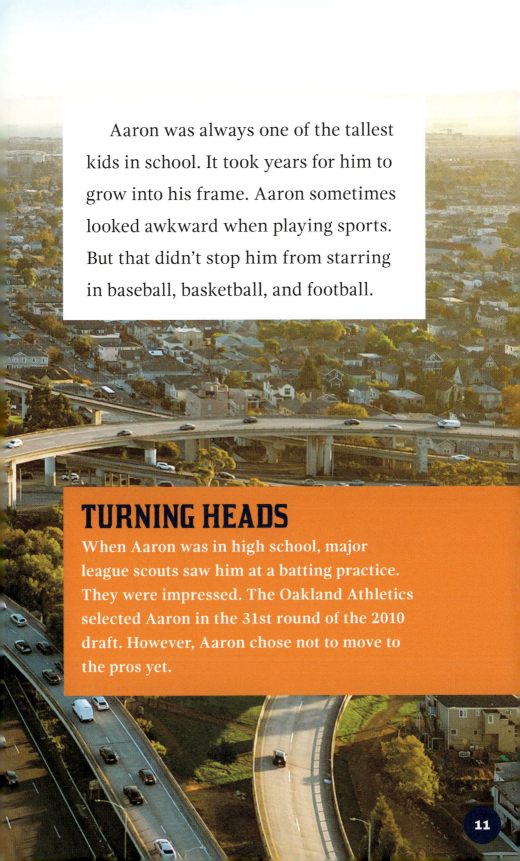

Aaron was always one of the tallest kids in school. It took years for him to grow into his frame. Aaron sometimes looked awkward when playing sports. But that didn't stop him from starring in baseball, basketball, and football.

TURNING HEADS

When Aaron was in high school, major league scouts saw him at a batting practice. They were impressed. The Oakland Athletics selected Aaron in the 31st round of the 2010 draft. However, Aaron chose not to move to the pros yet.

After high school, Aaron Judge attended college at nearby Fresno State. The young slugger was still growing when he got to college. By the end of his freshman year, he was 6-foot-7 (201 cm).

FOOTBALL OFFERS

Many big colleges had wanted Judge to join their football teams. Notre Dame, Stanford, and UCLA offered him football scholarships. But Judge turned them all down. He wanted to play baseball.

12

Fresno State's mascot is a bulldog.

Judge had 76 hits in the 2013 season.

Judge hit only six homers in his first two college seasons. But he worked hard to improve. The work paid off in his junior year. Judge led Fresno State with 12 home runs and 36 runs batted in (RBIs). He also had 12 steals. Scouts loved Judge's all-around game. He became a top MLB prospect.

A GREAT SUMMER

In 2012, Judge played in the Cape Cod Baseball League. This league is for top college players. Judge starred with five home runs. He also won his team's Citizenship Award. That is awarded for being a great teammate.

CHAPTER 3

ROAD TO THE MAJORS

After his junior year of college, Judge decided he was ready to move on. The New York Yankees selected him in the first round of the 2013 draft.

Aaron Judge was the 32nd overall pick of the 2013 draft.

To gain experience, Judge started out in the minor leagues. However, he injured his leg and missed the 2013 season. Judge returned to the field in 2014. Soon, he was smashing hits at the Class A level. He ended the season with 17 home runs. Yankees fans started to get excited about the up-and-coming star.

THE MINOR LEAGUES

Most MLB players have to work their way up through several minor league levels. The highest level is Triple A. Double A and Class A are below that. There are also lower leagues for rookies.

In 2014, Judge played for two of the Yankees' Class A teams. One was in Florida. The other was in South Carolina.

In 2015, Judge moved up to the Yankees' Double A team. That team was called the Trenton Thunder. The competition was tougher in Double A. But Judge was ready. He hit a three-run homer in his first game with the Thunder. He belted a total of 12 home runs in 63 games with the team. The Yankees decided Judge was ready for an even bigger challenge. In June, he moved up to Triple A.

In 2015, Judge had 71 hits and 44 RBIs for the Trenton Thunder.

Judge was one step away from his MLB dream. But the rising star had to get used to the talented Triple A pitchers. For the rest of 2015, Judge hit only .224 with 8 home runs. Judge also struck out a lot. The Yankees decided he wasn't ready for the big leagues yet.

FUTURES GAME

Each year, the minor league's best players face off in the All-Star Futures Game. Judge competed in the game in 2015. He got on base as a designated hitter. Then he scored a run. He helped his team win 10–1.

In the All-Star Futures Game, the best US players faced the best players from the rest of the world.

Judge spent the winter of 2015–16 working with a hitting coach. The slugger was soon swinging faster and harder than ever. He also practiced making better decisions at the plate. He wanted to avoid swinging at pitches outside the strike zone. Back in Triple A, Judge raised his batting average to .270. He hit 19 homers in 93 games. In August, the Yankees called Judge up to the majors.

In 2016, Judge tallied 65 RBIs for the Yankees' Triple A team.

IN THE SPOTLIGHT

A GRAND ENTRANCE

Aaron Judge had an impressive first MLB game. In the first inning, he showed off his fielding skills. A towering pop fly headed toward the fence. Judge sprinted across right field. He made a running catch for the third out. Next, Judge showed off his skills at the plate. His first at-bat came in the second inning. Judge smashed a homer over center field. The next day, Judge homered again.

AARON JUDGE PLAYED HIS FIRST MLB GAME ON AUGUST 13, 2016.

He became just the second Yankee to hit home runs in each of his first two games.

CHAPTER 4

TOP TALENT

Judge struggled through the rest of the 2016 season. He struck out in nearly half of his at-bats. He hit just .179 for the year. Then, Judge hurt his back in September. His season came to an early end.

Judge played only 27 MLB games in 2016.

Judge hit 24 doubles in the 2017 season.

30

Judge hadn't played much in 2016. So, he was still considered a rookie in 2017. Soon, he got back to blasting home runs. Judge recorded 27 homers by the end of June. Fans were impressed. Judge earned a spot in the All-Star Game.

DEEP BOMB

On September 30, 2017, Judge hit a monster home run. The ball cleared the left-field seats at Yankee Stadium. The home run measured 496 feet (151 m). That was the longest home run of the 2017 MLB season.

On July 7, 2017, Judge hit his 30th home run of the year. That set the record for most home runs by a Yankee rookie. And the team's newest superstar wasn't done putting his name in the record book. On September 25, Judge hit two more homers. That put him at 50 for the year. It was a new MLB record for rookies.

OFF THE CHARTS

MLB uses sensors and computer programs to track the speed and distance of each hit. On July 21, 2017, Judge crushed a home run in Seattle. He hit the ball so hard that the tracking program couldn't record it.

In 2017, Judge broke an MLB rookie home run record that had stood since 1987.

The Yankees made the playoffs in 2017. In the fourth inning of the AL Wild Card Game, Judge whacked a line drive over the left-field fence. The two-run homer helped New York win 8–4.

Judge had nine hits in the 2017 playoffs. Three of them were doubles. Four more were home runs. The Yankees were one game away from the World Series. But they fell to the Houston Astros in a heartbreaking Game 7 loss.

Judge racked up 11 RBIs during the 2017 playoffs.

In 2017, Judge became the first rookie to lead the majors in home runs, runs, and walks.

After the 2017 season, Judge was named AL Rookie of the Year. Every voter picked him. Judge also finished second in voting for the Most Valuable Player (MVP) Award.

THE JUDGE'S CHAMBERS

Yankees fans loved to cheer for Aaron Judge. Some dressed up as courtroom judges. They sat in a special section in right field. It was decorated to look like a courtroom. Fans called it the Judge's Chambers.

CHAPTER 5

MAKING HISTORY

Judge got off to a hot start in 2018. By late July, he'd hit 26 home runs. But then he injured his wrist. Judge didn't come back until late in the season. He hit three home runs in his first three playoff games. However, the Boston Red Sox knocked the Yankees out of the playoffs.

In 2018, Judge had 115 hits in just 112 games.

Another injury forced Judge to miss two months in 2019. And in 2020, the season was shortened to 60 games due to the COVID-19 pandemic. Judge played in only 28 of those games.

CENTER-FIELD TOWER

In 2018, Judge started playing some games at center field. Usually, center fielders are a baseball team's fastest athletes. The assignment showed Judge's all-around skill.

Judge tied the MLB record for the tallest starting center fielder.

In 2021, Judge finally had another healthy year. He got right back to his power-hitting ways. That season, Judge notched 39 home runs. And he brought his batting average up to .287. The Yankees also made it to the playoffs. They faced the Boston Red Sox in the AL Wild Card Game. However, New York lost 6–2.

Judge had 158 hits in 2021.

In 2022, Judge became the sixth player in MLB history to hit 60 or more homers in one season.

Judge started strong in 2022. The Yankees faced the Toronto Blue Jays on May 10. In the ninth inning, Judge crushed a three-run homer. The Yankees won 6–5. It was Judge's first walk-off home run. The slugger didn't stop there. He hit his 61st homer on September 28. That tied the all-time AL record. And on October 4, Judge broke the mark.

MONEY BALL

A fan named Cory Youmans caught Judge's historic home run. In the winter of 2022, Youmans brought the ball to an auction. It sold for $1.5 million.

The Yankees once again made the playoffs in 2022. But Judge struggled. He struck out 15 times in the postseason. In nine playoff games, Judge had only five hits. The Houston Astros ended New York's season. After the playoffs, Judge was named AL MVP. However, he was frustrated to be stopped short of the World Series.

TRIPLE THREAT

A player wins the Triple Crown if he leads the league in batting average, home runs, and RBIs. Judge barely missed it in 2022. He was first in homers and RBIs. But he ended the season just five points behind the batting-average leader.

In 2022, the Yankees won the AL East with a record of 99–63.

IN THE SPOTLIGHT

WALK-OFF CLINCHER

On October 3, 2021, the Yankees faced the Tampa Bay Rays. The score was tied 0–0 in the ninth inning. Two Yankees were on base. Then, Judge stepped up to the plate. He swung at a low pitch. The ball bounced toward second base. Teammate Tyler Wade sprinted down the third-base line. Wade slid across home plate for a run. That gave Judge the first walk-off hit of his

JUDGE'S WALK-OFF SINGLE GAVE THE YANKEES A 1–0 VICTORY.

career. More importantly, the win clinched a playoff spot for New York. The Yankees dugout emptied onto the field to celebrate with Judge.

CHAPTER 6
ALL RISE

Judge became a free agent after the 2022 season. Many teams offered him deals. One of them was the San Francisco Giants. The Giants are based near Judge's hometown. But Judge decided to stay with the Yankees. He became the highest-paid player in MLB history.

In 2022, Judge agreed to stay with the Yankees for nine more years.

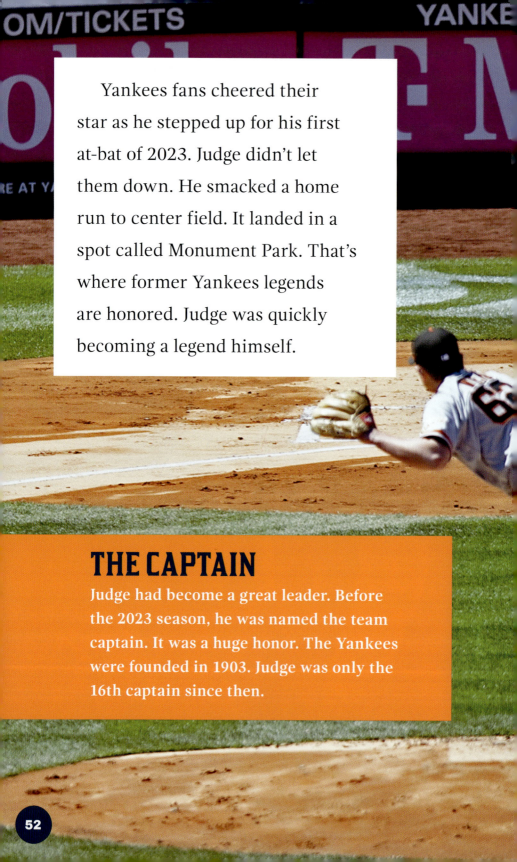

Yankees fans cheered their star as he stepped up for his first at-bat of 2023. Judge didn't let them down. He smacked a home run to center field. It landed in a spot called Monument Park. That's where former Yankees legends are honored. Judge was quickly becoming a legend himself.

THE CAPTAIN

Judge had become a great leader. Before the 2023 season, he was named the team captain. It was a huge honor. The Yankees were founded in 1903. Judge was only the 16th captain since then.

Judge's 422-foot (129-m) homer lifted the Yankees to a 5–0 win on Opening Day.

Judge led MLB with 144 RBIs in 2024.

Judge got off to a slow start in 2024. But his play picked up by the late summer. On August 14, Judge played in the 955th game of his career. That day, he hit his 300th homer. No player had ever reached that mark so fast.

OFF THE FIELD

After the 2023 season, Judge received the Roberto Clemente Award. That award honors players who do great work for their communities. Judge won it for his ALL RISE Foundation. The organization teaches leadership skills to kids.

In 2024, Judge had his second MVP season. He led thc Yankees to a division crown. Then, the team cruised through the playoffs. However, New York lost to the Los Angeles Dodgers in the World Series. Despite the loss, Yankees fans had high hopes for the future. They looked forward to cheering on Judge for years to come.

EXCLUSIVE CLUB

Judge hit 58 home runs in 2024. It was his third season with more than 50 homers. Only four players had done that before. They were Babe Ruth, Mark McGwire, Sammy Sosa, and Alex Rodriguez.

56

Judge hit a home run in Game 5 of the 2024 World Series.

TIMELINE

1992 — Aaron Judge is born on April 26 in Linden, California.

2010 — Judge joins the baseball team at Fresno State.

2013 — The New York Yankees select Judge in the first round of the MLB Draft.

2016 — Judge hits a home run in his first major league at-bat.

2017 — Judge breaks an MLB record by hitting 52 home runs as a rookie.

2021

Judge makes the All-Star team for the first time since 2018.

2022

Judge sets a new AL record by hitting 62 home runs in a season. He also wins his first MVP Award.

2022

In December, Judge signs a nine-year deal with the Yankees.

2024

In October, Judge leads New York to the World Series.

2024

In November, Judge wins his second MVP Award.

COMPREHENSION QUESTIONS

Write your answers on a separate piece of paper.

1. Write a paragraph that explains the main ideas of Chapter 4.

2. Which of Aaron Judge's records do you think is most impressive? Why?

3. Which team did the Yankees play in the 2024 World Series?
   A. San Francisco Giants
   B. Oakland Athletics
   C. Los Angeles Dodgers

4. For how many seasons did Aaron Judge play in the minor leagues?
   A. one season
   B. three seasons
   C. six seasons

5. What does **prospect** mean in this book?

Scouts loved Judge's all-around game.
*He became a top MLB **prospect**.*

    A. a player who is expected to do well at a higher level

    B. a person who looks for talented new players

    C. a player who most scouts have not heard of

6. What does **assignment** mean in this book?

*In 2018, Judge started playing some games at center field. Usually, center fielders are a baseball team's fastest athletes. The **assignment** showed Judge's all-around skill.*

    A. number

    B. job

    C. speed

Answer key on page 64.

GLOSSARY

adopted
Raised by people who are not a child's birth parents.

designated hitter
A baseball player who bats in place of a pitcher.

division
A group of teams within a league.

draft
A system that lets teams select new players coming into the league.

free agent
A professional athlete who doesn't have a contract with a team and is free to sign with any team.

pandemic
A time when a disease spreads quickly around the world.

playoffs
A set of games played after the regular season to decide which team is the champion.

rookies
Athletes in their first year as professional players.

scholarships
Money given to students to help pay for college.

scouts
People who travel around to look for new, talented players.

steroid
Drugs that increase strength and endurance.

TO LEARN MORE

BOOKS

Flynn, Brendan. *New York Yankees All-Time Greats*. Press Box Books, 2021.

Hewson, Anthony K. *Aaron Judge*. Abdo Publishing, 2024.

Pettiford, Rebecca. *Aaron Judge*. Bellwether Media, 2024.

ONLINE RESOURCES

Visit **www.apexeditions.com** to find links and resources related to this title.

ABOUT THE AUTHOR

Charlie Beattie is a writer and former sportscaster. Originally from Saint Paul, Minnesota, he now lives in Charleston, South Carolina, with his wife and son.

INDEX

All-Star Futures Game, 22
All-Star Game, 31
American League (AL), 6, 34, 37, 42, 45–46

Boston Red Sox, 38, 42

Cape Cod Baseball League, 15
Class A, 18

Double A, 18, 20

Fresno State, 12, 15

Houston Astros, 34, 46

Linden, California, 9
Los Angeles Dodgers, 56

McGwire, Mark, 56
minor leagues, 18, 22
Monument Park, 52
Most Valuable Player (MVP), 37, 46, 56

National League (NL), 6

Oakland Athletics, 11

playoffs, 34, 38, 42, 46, 48, 56

Roberto Clemente Award, 55
Rodriguez, Alex, 56
Ruth, Babe, 56

San Francisco Giants, 50
Sosa, Sammy, 56

Tampa Bay Rays, 48
Toronto Blue Jays, 45
Trenton Thunder, 20
Triple A, 18, 20, 22, 24
Triple Crown, 46

Wade, Tyler, 48
World Series, 34, 46, 56

Yankee Stadium, 31
Youmans, Cory, 45

ANSWER KEY:

1. Answers will vary; 2. Answers will vary; 3. C; 4. B; 5. A; 6. B